Getting To Know...

Nature's Children

TURTLES

Merebeth Switzer

Grolier

Facts in Brief

Classification of North American turtles

    Class: *Reptilia* (reptiles)

    Order: *Testudines*

    Family: 7 main families; the largest in North America is *Emydidae* (family of sub-aquatic turtles) which contains 8 genera and 26 species

    Genus: 19 genera of turtles are found in North America

    Species: Approximately 50 North American species

World distribution. Varies with species.

Habitat. Varies with species.

Distinctive physical characteristics. Protective shell covers body; hard toothless beak.

Habits. Lays its eggs on land, and most species bury them.

Diet. Varies with species.

Edited by: Elizabeth Grace Zuraw
Design/Photo Editor: Nancy Norton
Photo Rights: Ivy Images

ISBN: 0-7172-8774-2

Have you ever wondered . . .

if mother turtles look after their babies	page 6
who a turtle's relatives are?	page 9
where in North America turtles live?	page 10
if sea turtles come ashore?	page 12
if turtles have claws?	page 13
what a turtle's shell is made of?	page 16
how the Stinkpot got its name?	page 19
if turtles can run?	page 20
how some turtles can stay underwater so long?	page 23
if turtles can blink?	page 24
if turtles have favorite foods?	page 27
if a turtle can stick out its tongue?	page 28
if turtles make any sounds?	page 31
how a turtle may attract a mate?	page 31
what turtles do all day?	page 32
how turtles warm themselves up after a chilly night?	page 32
how turtles keep cool in hot weather?	page 35
if turtles build homes?	page 35
where turtles sleep?	page 35
what turtles do in winter?	page 36
where mother turtles lay their eggs?	page 39
how many eggs a mother turtle may lay?	page 40
how long it takes turtle eggs to hatch?	page 43
how long turtles live?	page 46
Words To Know	page 47
Index	page 48

Alligator Snapping Turtles, such as the one shown here, are among the largest turtles in North America.

If you could look back in time and see the Earth as it appeared 200 million years ago, you'd see giant trees, strange plants, and dinosaurs. But wait, what's that? Why, it's a turtle. That's right. There were turtles way back in the days of the dinosaurs. And amazingly, they've changed very little since that time.

Maybe that's why turtles have fascinated people and why there are so many stories and legends about them. You almost certainly know at least one turtle story: Aesop's fable about the Tortoise that races the Hare—and wins! But did you know that ancient legends from places as far apart as China, North America, and India say that the Earth is carried on the back of a turtle?

Do turtles deserve their reputation for slowness as well as determination? And how did they survive so much longer than their ancient friends? Read on to learn more about these amazing creatures.

Wise Young Turtles

Imagine a long, wide stretch of empty beach. It's the middle of the night, and the moon and stars are out.

Opposite page: *All turtles lay their eggs on land. After hatching, this baby sea turtle makes its way to the sea.*

Look over there, where the sand meets the trees. Can you see that the sand seems to be moving? Watch carefully now…isn't that a little dark spot, just there? It's moving this way, toward the water.…And there's another one behind it, and another.

What can they be, these tiny crawling shapes coming up out of the sand?

They are turtle *hatchlings,* babies born from eggs. But where did they come from, where are they going, and why are they out here alone?

One of the truly amazing things about turtles is that they are born knowing almost everything they need to know to cope with the world on their own. Once their mother has prepared their nest, laid her eggs, and covered them carefully, she has done all she needs to do for her babies.

*Loggerhead Turtles can weigh up to 300 pounds
(130 kilograms). Their shells sometimes grow to
the size of a small rowboat.*

Reptile Relatives

Turtles are *reptiles*. This means they are relatives of crocodiles, snakes, and lizards. All reptiles have certain features in common. For one thing, although some spend a great deal of time in the water, they must breathe air through lungs, just as you do.

What else do reptiles have in common? Think carefully. Have you ever seen a furry snake or a turtle with eyelashes? No? That's because reptiles don't have hair. Instead, they have a thick scaly or leathery covering.

Finally, reptiles are *cold-blooded,* they have no built-in temperature control. While your body always stays at more or less the same temperature no matter how cold or hot the weather, a reptile's does not. Its temperature goes up when it's in the sun and down when it moves into the shade.

As you can imagine, this affects how and where reptiles, including turtles, live.

Turtle Territory

Turtles are found almost anywhere that's warm for at least several months of the year. Even though they depend on their surroundings to keep their body at the right temperature, turtles have ways of surviving the cold winters. But in between they need a good period of summer warmth and sunshine.

In North America this means that turtles can live all through the United States and Mexico, but only in the southern part of Canada. Some types, such as Painted and Snapping Turtles, are found in many regions. Others are found only in one small area. The Yellow Blotch Map Turtle, for instance, lives only in one part of Mississippi.

To warm their bodies, these Painted Turtles line up on a log to catch some of the sun's rays.

What's in a Name

You have probably heard someone call turtles *tortoises*. And you may have run into yet another name for turtles—*terrapin*.

Fortunately, this is not really as confusing as it may seem. There are many different kinds of turtles, but they fall into three main categories: sea turtles, tortoises or land turtles, and fresh-water turtles, sometimes called terrapins. But whatever they're called, they're all turtles.

Who's Who

Sea turtles are found in the Atlantic and the Pacific Oceans and in the Gulf of Mexico. Their legs are flattened, paddle-like flippers, and they spend almost all their time in the water. They come ashore only to lay their eggs. Most sea turtles are very large. Many grow to be more than 220 pounds (100 kilograms).

Tortoises are turtles that can live only on land. They are poor swimmers and usually live near deserts and grasslands. You can spot them by their stump-like legs and their high, rounded shells.

Although some turtles spend their entire lives on land, most spend part of their time in the water and part on land. The turtles you probably know best are the freshwater turtles you might find near your home or cottage or on special country outings. These turtles spend part of their time in the water of lakes, ponds, and streams, and part on land. They have many different styles of shells and their feet are usually suited for both walking and swimming. Most of these turtles have claws, and some of those that spend a great deal of time in the water have *webbed feet,* feet with toes joined together by flaps of skin.

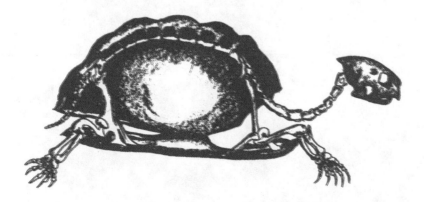

Its firmly attached shell is part of a turtle's body. The turtle could not survive without its shell.

Built-in Armor

If you were asked to describe a turtle, where would you start? With its shell, of course. After all, to most of us, that's what makes a turtle a turtle.

But turtle shells can look very different. They may be high and rounded, like those of the tortoise. Or they may be low and sleek and streamlined, like those of turtles that spend time in the water. Or they may be any style in between.

Turtle shells may be brown or green all over or a mottled mixture of dullish shades. Or they may have brightly colored spots, streaks, borders, or intricate patterns.

But whatever a turtle's shell looks like, it is bony and hard and it's the turtle's main means of protection. Many turtles can pull their head, tail, and legs inside their shell—and they do so at the first hint of danger.

This built-in armor may be one of the reasons that turtles have survived for so many generations.

Opposite page:
The faint yellow lines on its shell give the Map Turtle its name.

A Box Turtle has a large hinged plastron and can withdraw completely into its shell.

Snapping Turtles have very small plastrons and cannot pull their head and legs inside.

Upside/Downside

A turtle's shell has two parts—a top called the *carapace* and a bottom called the *plastron.* The parts are usually joined at the sides by bony ridges. At the front and back ends are openings for the turtle's head, tail, and chunky legs.

Both parts of a turtle's shell have an inner layer made up of bony plates that are actually part of the turtle's backbone and ribs. Covering this on most turtles is a layer of broad, thin scales called *scutes,* made of material something like your fingernails.

Sometimes a turtle may have sharp points or other strange looking lumps on its back. These are scutes specially grown to help the turtle look threatening or blend into its surroundings.

Some turtles shed their scutes as they grow, but new ones are already formed underneath. That way the turtle is never without protection.

The Blanding's Turtle has a hinged plastron.

Stinky Stinkpot

Most grown-up turtles have shells that are strong enough to keep them pretty safe. Babies, however, and some other kinds of turtles are so small that their shells don't pose much of a problem for *predators,* animals that hunt other animals for food.

But some small turtles have another special safety device. The Stinkpot Turtle and its close relatives, the Mud and Musk Turtles, can produce a strong smelly liquid called *musk.* When these turtles arc disturbed, they release this unpleasant musk all over the intruder. A close encounter with a Stinkpot would show you that its name is well deserved!

Common Musk Turtle is another name for the Stinkpot. Though small, this turtle's mighty smell gives it its nickname.

Clumsy on Land

Turtles are famous for their slowness, and it's true that most of them do poke along awkwardly on land.

Strangely enough, tortoises—the turtles that live entirely on land—are particularly clumsy on their stumpy legs and small feet. No wonder Aesop's Hare thought it had nothing to worry about in its race with the Tortoise!

Freshwater turtles move more quickly on land than most tortoises. Some can even run— though not what you'd call *fast*—and some can climb. The Stinkpot, for example, can climb the trunks of small trees to a height of more than 6 feet (2 meters).

Nonetheless, most freshwater and all sea turtles move most easily in the water. They can swim quite fast, and large sea turtles can cover great distances to find food. Female sea turtles may *migrate,* or travel, thousands of miles (kilometers) to return to the nesting sites where they themselves hatched to lay their own eggs.

*Tasty treats for the Desert Tortoise are the plants
and flowers that sprout when occasional rain
causes the desert to bloom.*

Green sea turtles can swim up to 20 miles (32 kilometers) an hour for short periods. At that rate, this turtle can outswim human divers.

Lung Power

A turtle breathes through its mouth and nose and uses lungs, just as you do. However, it does have one difficulty.

If you place your hand on your chest, you'll feel your ribs moving, helping you to breathe. But a turtle's ribs, being fixed to its shell, cannot move. A turtle's body, however, is specially built so that it can make its lungs expand simply by moving its legs.

Even though many turtles spend a lot of time underwater, they still need to breathe. Some have ways for their bodies to take in small amounts of oxygen directly from the water. Others have a long, snorkel-like nose that allows them to keep their body underwater while they breathe oxygen from the air. And all of them can slow down their heartbeat when they are underwater, so that their body needs less oxygen. How long they can stay underwater without coming up for air depends on the *species,* or kind, of turtle—and on what it's doing. A swimming turtle uses up oxygen much faster than a turtle at rest.

Turtle Senses

Turtles do not have the same kind of ears as you. A turtle's ears are flat against its head and are really pieces of skin stretched over the ear opening. People used to think that turtles could not hear sounds but could only feel them through their body. We now know that a turtle can actually hear as well as a cat. Some owners of pet turtles even claim that their pet will come when they call.

Turtles see quite well, too. Unlike many animals, they can see colors and seem to be particularly sensitive to red. And unlike their cousins the snakes, turtles have moveable eye-lids and can blink.

Don't worry if you see a turtle gulping air. It's not having trouble breathing. It's simply bringing air into its mouth in order to smell its surroundings and sniff out its next meal.

The Eastern Painted Turtle, though common, is shy and difficult to approach.

Turtle Treats

Speaking of meals, what do turtles like to eat? That depends on the type of turtle and the kinds of food available.

Opposite page: *To avoid the hot sun, the Desert Tortoise feeds in the early morning or late afternoon.*

Some types of turtles, especially the tortoises, feed mainly on plants. They are called *herbivores.* Other types eat only meat. They are called *carnivores.* The Snapping Turtle is a carnivore. It feeds on insects, crayfish, crabs, snails, fish, frogs, toads, snakes, birds' eggs, and small mammals.

Most turtles, however, are *omnivores,* they eat plants as well as animals. They do have favorite foods, though, and so we're fairly sure they have a keen sense of taste. The Leatherback Turtle, for example, has a definite passion for jellyfish, while the Green Sea Turtle prefers eel grass.

Most turtles can go for days or even weeks without eating. But when food is plentiful, they'll eat all they can and may become quite fat.

Toothless Jaws, Tempting Tongues

To munch all this food you would think that a turtle must have a pretty good set of teeth. Not so. In fact, turtles have no teeth at all! They do, however, have a hard beak that has a rough cutting edge used for tearing apart and sometimes grinding their food. Some turtles, such as the Alligator Snapping Turtle, have such a strong beak that they could easily cut a fish in half—and possibly chomp off a person's finger. With all Snapping Turtles, it's best to let an expert handle them.

A turtle can't stick out its tongue, but it does have one. It uses its tongue to move food around in its mouth and into its throat. The Alligator Snapping Turtle even has an extra tongue-like growth in its mouth that looks rather like a worm. When the turtle holds its mouth open and wiggles this "tongue," it acts like a fishing lure. Soon an unwary fish swims in, expecting dinner. Instead, the fish becomes a tasty tidbit for the turtle.

Opposite page:
An Alligator Snapping Turtle opens its mouth to reveal the worm-like structure on its tongue.

Turtle Talk

Turtles are basically quiet creatures. They live pretty much on their own, and most of them don't have special areas they protect from other turtles. This means that they really have little need to communicate with each other.

Turtles do make sounds, however. An angry turtle, especially a young one, will often hiss loudly at an attacker. And some turtles may grunt, while others have a whistling call that they seem to produce mainly in *mating season,* the time of year during which animals come together to produce young.

When trying to attract or impress a female, some male turtles use silent body language to get their message across. Some wave their long toenails in the female's face, while others have special ways of bobbing their heads.

A Blanding's Turtle pokes only its nose into the air to breathe, keeping the rest of its body underwater.

31

Passing the Time

Like most animals in the wild, turtles spend a good deal of their waking hours looking for food. Some do this mainly at night, others in the daytime, still others at dawn or dusk.

Because turtles cannot control the temperature of their bodies, most of them spend as much time as they can basking in the sun. They must do so to warm themselves up after a long swim or a chilly night.

If you watch carefully when you are near a pond or marsh on a sunny day, you may see a turtle basking on a log or rock with its neck and legs stretched out and its toes spread wide apart. The turtle is trying to catch as much of the sun's warmth as possible. In fact, you may see several turtles sunning themselves. Sometimes, if good sunning space is scarce, you might even see one turtle sprawled on top of a larger one's shell!

The Florida Cooter usually stays in the water but occasionally comes out to warm itself in the sun.

Keeping Cool

Turtles can get *too* hot, however, so they must not wander far from water or from trees, plants or rocks. That way, if a turtle feels too hot while sunbathing, it can simply move into the shade. Or it can dunk itself in the water—just as you might if you were lying on a hot beach and wanted to cool off.

But if turtles can get too hot, how do the tortoises of the southwestern United States cope with the high temperatures of the desert?

They survive by digging *burrows,* or underground homes. A burrow is much cooler and more moist than the open desert. Deep in the ground, a tortoise can keep cool and save the precious water its body contains. On very hot days the tortoise might not come out of its burrow at all.

Tortoises are the only turtles that build any form of home. All other turtles simply make use of the world around them. A sleepy turtle may snooze at the bottom of a marsh, doze under a log, or snuggle down into the mud of a pond.

Opposite page: *On a hot day, a dip in the water cools off this Snapping Turtle.*

Sleeping away the Winter

Turtles in northern areas would freeze if they couldn't find a way to avoid winter. So, like some other animals, they *hibernate,* or go into a kind of deep sleep during the winter.

As fall approaches and the weather begins to cool, these turtles start to put on extra fat. This will supply what energy they need through the winter. As the temperature drops still more, they gradually get less and less active. Finally they nestle deep into the mud at the bottom of ponds or into the loose soil of the forest floor and settle in to sleep the winter away.

Scientists have found that the blood of hibernating turtles actually changes to work rather like the antifreeze that people buy in winter for their cars. As a result, the turtle's body temperature can drop to only a few degrees above freezing—much lower than that of most animals that hibernate.

In the spring, as soil or water begins to warm, the turtle's body, too, gradually warms up. Finally the turtle awakens, ready to take on another year.

Early warm spells in winter can be dangerous for turtles. If they wake up too soon from their winter sleep, a return to cold weather could catch them unprepared and they might freeze. In fact, winter can be the biggest danger a turtle faces in its adult life.

Nesting Time

Different types of turtles have their young at different ages. Mud Turtles are about 5 or 6 years old when they mate, while the Desert Tortoise must wait until it is about 15 years old. Some turtles nest one or more times a year, while others may nest only once every few years. A turtle that nests once a year usually lays its eggs in the spring so that the eggs will be kept warm by the heat of the summer sun.

All turtles bury their eggs in sand or soil. Even sea turtles come ashore and drag themselves a few hundred yards (meters) onto the beach to lay their eggs.

Many turtles have traditional nesting grounds that have been used for generations. The mother's *instinct,* or strong natural desire, is to lay her eggs in a certain place. This can be dangerous because she tries to cross any barrier, including backyards, fences, and busy highways, to reach her nesting ground. Turtles are often hit by cars as they cross roads on their way to lay their eggs.

Opposite page:
A few kinds of turtles, including this softshell turtle, have a hard leathery skin over their shell, which gives them a sleeker, smooth look.

As Safe as Mom Can Make Them

The mother turtle usually lays her eggs in the middle of the night. This is the safest time for turtles to be out in the open.

First she digs a hole with her hind feet, using her front legs to hold her body in place. After the hole is dug she holds her body over the nest and deposits her eggs in it.

Depending on the species of turtle, the mother may lay one to several hundred eggs. She then covers the nest and packs down the loose soil with her body. She may pack the soil for quite a distance around the nest. This helps to confuse hungry predators as to the exact location of a possible dinner.

A female Snapping Turtle may lay as many as 50 eggs before she is finished.

On Their Own

A turtle mother never sees her babies. She leaves her eggs to hatch in the warmth of the sun. It takes two or more months for the eggs to develop. During this time, the leathery roundish eggs may be found and eaten by foxes, skunks, bears, raccoons, or other animals. The nest may also be flooded during heavy rains and the eggs may be washed away. Or the eggs may dry out if they are not buried deep enough. But most turtle mothers lay many eggs, which helps insure that at least some babies will survive.

The Yellow Mud Turtle, found in the United States, is a freshwater species that grows to a length of about 6 inches (15 centimeters).

The Long Trek

When a baby turtle is ready to hatch, it must break through the tough shell of its egg. To do this, each hatchling uses a special growth on its beak. Called an *egg tooth,* it helps crack open the egg.

Once the baby is out of its shell, it climbs up through the soil or sand to the land surface. Some lucky hatchlings find themselves in or near a suitable place to live. But many young water turtles must undertake a long journey. Even if they can't see the water, they know instinctively in which direction to go. One after another they set out across the stretch of sand or through the woods to find the ocean, marsh, or pond their mother came from.

This is another dangerous time for young turtles. Hawks, gulls, raccoons, skunks, and even fish see the tiny hatchlings as an easy meal. But the babies seem to know this, too. They usually surface only after dark when they're less likely to be spotted by predators.

This baby Snapping Turtle broke out of its shell with the help of an egg tooth, a growth that falls off within a few days of the hatching.

From Small Beginnings

All turtle hatchlings are about the size of a quarter. It's hard to believe that some of these tiny creatures may someday grow up to be giant Leatherback Sea Turtles weighing more than 1,500 pounds (700 kilograms) and measuring nearly 8 feet (2.5 meters) in length. In fact, some Leatherbacks have weighed more than 2,200 pounds (1,000 kilograms)!

The smaller species of turtles may live up to 5 years; the larger ones live much longer. There are many stories of turtles that are even more than 100 years old.

Today people are one of the biggest threats to the survival of turtles. People drive cars that kill countless turtles on the roads. People also create pollution and expand cities into natural areas, destroying places where turtles live. Other people kill turtles for their beautiful shells and food.

The earliest turtles lived more than 185 million years ago. If these amazing reptiles are to continue their long history, people need to make greater efforts to save them.

Words To Know

Burrow An animal's underground home.

Carapace A turtle's top shell.

Carnivore An animal that eats mainly meat.

Cold-blooded Having a body temperature that stays about the same as the surrounding air or water.

Egg tooth Point on a baby turtle's beak to break open its shell.

Hatchling A baby produced from an egg.

Herbivore An animal that eats mainly plants.

Hibernation A kind of sleep that some animals take in winter.

Instinct A strong, inborn pattern of behavior.

Mating season The time of year during which animals mate, or come together to produce young.

Migrate To move from one place to another.

Musk A strong-smelling substance produced by some animals.

Omnivore An animal that eats both plants and animals.

Plastron A turtle's bottom shell.

Predator An animal that hunts other animals for food.

Reptiles A class of animals that are cold-blooded, hairless, and usually egg-laying, have scales, and breathe through lungs.

Scutes Scaly plates that cover a turtle's shell.

Species Class or kind of animals with certain traits in common.

Terrapins The name usually used to describe freshwater turtles.

Tortoise Turtles that live only on land. (In some countries, the word is commonly used for freshwater turtles, too).

Webbed feet Feet with toes joined by flaps of skin.

Index

Alligator Snapping Turtle, 28
armor, 15, 16, 46

babies: *see* hatchlings
beak, 28
body temperature, 9, 10, 32, 35, 36, 37
Box Turtle, 16
breathing, 23, 24

carapace, 16
claws, 13
communication, 31

danger, 37, 43, 44
Desert Tortoise, 35, 39
diet, 27, 28
digging, 40
dinosaurs, 5
distribution, 10

eggs, 6, 12, 20, 39, 40, 43, 44

female, 6, 20, 31, 39, 40, 43

Green Sea Turtle, 27

hatchlings, 6, 19, 40, 43, 44, 46
hibernation, 36
homes, 35

Leatherback Sea Turtle, 27, 46
legends, 5
legs, 12, 13, 20, 23, 40
life span, 46

lungs, 23

male, 31
Map Turtle, 10,
mating, 31, 39
migration, 20
Mud Turtle, 19, 39
Musk Turtle, 19

nesting, 39

Painted Turtle, 10,
plastron, 16

relatives, 9
reptiles, 9
ribs, 16, 23

scutes, 16
sea turtles, 12, 20
senses, 24
shell, 13, 15, 16, 19
size, 12, 19, 46
Snapping Turtle, 10, 16, 27
Stinkpot, 19, 20
summer, 10
sunbathing, 32, 35

terrapin, 12
tongue, 28
tortoise, 12, 13, 20, 35
types of turtles, 12

webbed feet, 13
winter, 10, 36, 37

PHOTO CREDITS
Cover: Bill Ivy. **Interiors:** *Ivy Images:* Dr. George K. Peck, 4, 8, 42-43; Robert McCaw, 11; Wayne Lynch, 21, 33. /Duane Sept, 7. /James Richards, 14. /Bill Ivy, 17, 25, 30, 34, 41, 45. /*Valan Photos:* Robert C. Simpson, 18. /*Earth Views / Ivy Images:* Ingrid Visser, 22. /Wayne Lynch, 26. /*Tom Stack & Associates:* Mary Clay, 29. /*Network Stock Photo File:* Brian Morin, 38.

Getting To Know...

Nature's Children

BEES

Elin Kelsey

Grolier

Facts in Brief

Classification of the Honeybee

    Class: *Insectae* (insects)

    Order: *Hymenoptera* (insects with membranous wings)

    Family: *Apidae* (bee family)

    Genus: *Apis*

    Species: *Apis mellifera* (honey-carrying bee)

World distribution. Honeybees live worldwide except in polar regions.

Habitat. Honeybees live wherever flowers provide sufficient food.

Distinctive physical characteristics. Thick round body with black and yellow stripes.

Habits. Social insect that lives in large colonies; well-established division of labor among workers, drones, and queens; uses dances to communicate location of flowers; aids in the pollination of flowers while looking for food; able to detect changes in weather through changes in air pressure.

Edited by: Elizabeth Grace Zuraw
Design/Photo Editor: Nancy Norton
Photo Rights: Ivy Images

ISBN: 0-7172-8775-0

Have you ever wondered . . .

what kind of honeybees might be in your garden?	page 5
how many legs a bee has?	page 6
if a bee has any bones?	page 6
if bees can see colors?	page 9
whether a bee can taste?	page 10
if there are times when bees won't leave their hive?	page 13
how bees keep warm on cold days?	page 14
how often a flying bee flaps its wings?	page 17
where bees build their honeycombs?	page 18
where bees get the wax for their honeycombs?	page 18
how to recognize the queen bee?	page 22
how to recognize a drone?	page 22
how long a queen bee lives?	page 22
how many eggs a queen bee lays?	page 26
how big honeybee eggs are?	page 29
what bee grubs eat?	page 29
how long it takes grubs to become adult bees?	page 30
what jobs a worker bee does?	page 32
how a bee gets the nectar out of a flower?	page 35
how hard a bee works to make a thimbleful of honey?	page 36
how bees help flowers grow?	page 39
how honeybees communicate with each other?	page 41
why a bee will sting?	page 45
Words To Know	page 47
Index	page 48

Bzzzz! A busy honeybee buzzes by you on its way through your garden or backyard. Did you know that without the labors of honeybees like this one, there wouldn't be any honey to put on your toast in the morning?

The bees that we see in fields and gardens are worker bees. They live in a *hive,* a bee home, that is organized a bit like a castle. Deep inside the hive lives its ruler, the *queen bee.* She is fed and guarded by thousands of female *worker bees.* Also living in the hive are the male bees, or *drones.*

There are more than 22,000 kinds of bees in the world, but only honeybees live in hives and produce large amounts of honey. Let's take a closer look at the hard-working honeybee and at life inside the hive.

Honeybees were not found in North America until the seventeenth century, when settlers brought them.

Bumblebee

Honeybee

Bee Basics

Everyone knows what a honeybee looks like. Its thick, round body and yellow and black stripes make it easy to spot. Insect-eating animals quickly learn that creatures sporting those stripes can pack a painful sting. In fact, a bee's stripes are such a good "stay away" warning that a few non-stinging insects have copied the striped pattern. These copycats, mistaken for bees, are left alone.

Like all insects, a bee has six legs and its body is made up of three parts. It has a round head, a middle section called a *thorax,* and an egg-shaped section on the end called an *abdomen.* Bees do not have bones. Instead, they have a hard outer "skin" called an *exoskeleton,* which supports their bodies from the outside.

Thanks to its resemblance to a honey- bee, this Beefly looks dangerous, but it couldn't sting even if it wanted to.

Sensitive Bee Senses

You find out about the world through your eyes, ears, nose, and fingers. A honeybee gets its information about what is happening in the world through its eyes, feelers, and body hairs.

The bee has two enormous eyes, each covering one whole side of its head. Each eye is divided into more than 4,000 tiny parts. When you see a flower, you see a single picture. But a bee probably sees a flower made up of thousands of little squares. Look at something through a fine wire screen and you'll get an idea of how a bee might see.

Bees cannot see the color red—to them it looks like black. But they can see other colors that you can't, just as dogs can hear sounds that you can't.

In addition to its two large eyes, a honeybee has three smaller eyes on top of its head. If you look carefully, you can see one of them on this bee.

A bee does not use a nose to smell as you do. Instead, it smells with a pair of long furry feelers called *antennae*. But these antennae do more than just smell. By sticking them into a jar of jam, for instance, a bee not only knows how the jam smells, but how it tastes and feels, too.

Bees also sense things through their hair. Each hair on a bee's fuzzy coat is as sensitive as a cat's whisker. These sensitive hairs help the honeybee to sense what is going on around it, particularly things that it cannot see. If an unfamiliar air current tickles its body hairs, the bee buzzes off.

The honeybee's sensitive antennae are constantly at work, smelling, feeling, and tasting everything they contact.

Weather Sense

If you're planning a picnic, keep an eye out for a bee "weather forecast." Lots of bees flying around means the weather will probably be fine for a picnic. If the bees have disappeared, think twice. You might be in for rain. But how do the bees know that? They know because they can detect changes in the air pressure. A sudden drop in air pressure tells bees that rain is on the way, and they don't leave their hive.

Rain isn't the only thing that keeps bees in their hive. If the temperature falls below 50 degrees Fahrenheit (10 degrees Celsius), you'll never see any bees. It's simply too cold for them to fly.

"Busy as a bee" and "hive of activity" are but two expressions that come from the hard-working and amazingly active honeybee.

Cold-weather Clusters

Like all insects, bees cannot completely control their body temperature. When they are outside, the temperature of their bodies is about as warm—or as cold—as the air around them. And the colder it gets, the more slowly the insects move. When it gets really cold, they can barely move at all, let alone fly.

On cold days, a *colony* of bees huddles inside its hive. A colony is a large group of bees or other animals. The bees on the cold outer edges of the hive try to push their way farther in to keep warm. By clustering in this way, bees can make their hive as warm as a summer afternoon, even when it's below freezing outside.

Thousands of clustering bees keep heat from escaping out of their hive.

Flying Aces

Sometimes in the summer a hive gets too hot. Then the bees use their built-in air conditioners to cool down their home. They simply flap their wings!

Every bee has two sets of wings—a large strong pair in the front and a small round pair behind those. When a bee flies, the front and hind wings hook together. These sets of wings always work together. Each wing is as thin and clear as a piece of plastic wrap. They may look too frail to lift a bee into the air, but don't be fooled. A honeybee can perform a most impressive air show.

For instance, if a worker bee suddenly spots a flower, it can turn in mid-air and dive in for a closer look. After hovering for a moment, it might zoom off and then up, perhaps as high as your bedroom ceiling, before flying on. Most amazing of all, in the time it takes you to blink, a flying bee flaps its wings 250 times!

Opposite page: *A worker honey-bee's powerful wings can carry her 3 miles (5 kilometers) in just 12 minutes.*

Honeycomb Hives

Opposite page:
In this close-up photo, the honey-comb cells look large. But there are about 25 cells in one square inch (6.5 square centimeters) of a honeycomb.

Many bees are kept by beekeepers who "farm" them for their honey. The beekeeper provides wooden boxes for the bees to build their hives in. Wild honeybees, however, must make their own homes. They build hives in hollow tree trunks or in rock crevices by glueing together thousands of tiny wax rooms called *cells.*

Believe it or not, all the wax used comes from the bees themselves. It is produced in special *glands* under their abdomens. A gland is a part of an animal's body that makes and gives out a substance. With their feet, the bees scoop tiny flakes of the wax into their mouths. Then, just as you would tackle a hard piece of bubble gum, the bees chew the wax to soften it. When it's soft, the bees use it to make the six-sided wax cells of the *honeycomb,* the name of the great mass of wax cells.

Most of the cells will be used for raising young worker bees and storing food. Slightly larger cells are built for the drones. And long thin cells are built for the queen bees.

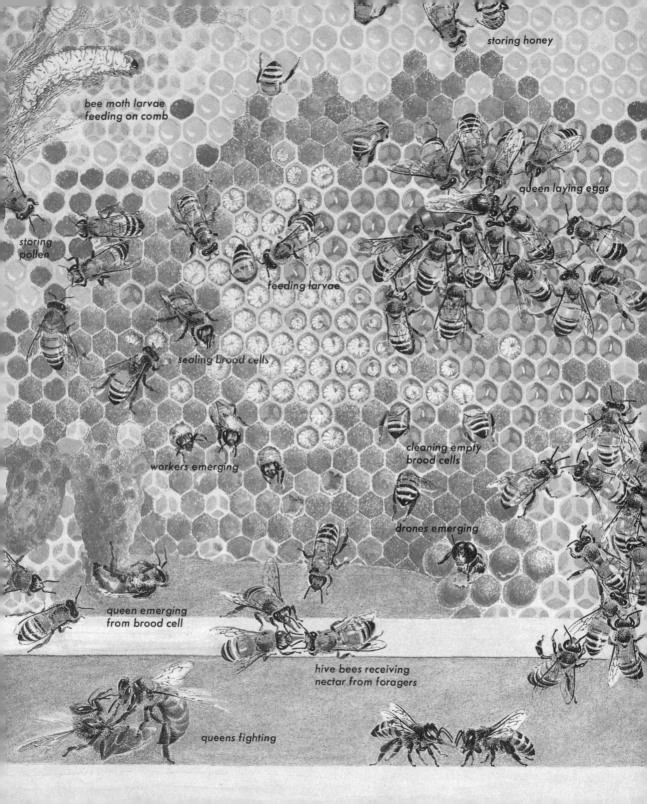

storing honey

bee moth larvae
feeding on comb

queen laying eggs

storing
pollen

feeding larvae

sealing brood cells

workers emerging

cleaning empty
brood cells

drones emerging

queen emerging
from brood cell

hive bees receiving
nectar from foragers

queens fighting

capping honey cells

scout performing
honey dance

building new
comb cells

ejecting drones

**ACTIVITIES INSIDE
A HONEYBEE HIVE**

fanning and guarding
the hive entrance

Jobs for Everyone

Each of the three types of honeybees has a special role in insuring the survival of the hive. All the hive-building work is done by the worker bees—and so is the housecleaning and food gathering. What then do the drones and the queen bee do?

A drone's job is to *mate* with the queen, or come together with her to produce young. The queen's job is to lay eggs so that there will always be new bees hatching.

The queen and the drones are larger than the worker bees. The queen is the longest member of her colony. She is also the skinniest. The drones are larger than the workers and the queen, and they have enormous eyes that cover most of the top of their heads.

The queen and drone bees rarely leave the hive. When they do, they fly much higher than the worker bees, so we rarely see them.

Size comparison

Queen

Worker

Drone

The queen bee, shown here in the center marked with a white spot, will live about two or three years.

Moving Houses

A new hive is started when an older hive gets too large. Somehow the queen bee instinctively knows it is time for her to find new quarters. But before she leaves the old hive, she lays eggs in the long thin cells specially built for producing queens. The eggs are called *royal eggs* because they will grow into queen bees. These queen eggs are fed a special baby food called *royal jelly.*

When the new queens begin to hatch, the old queen can leave. She sends out scouts to find a new place for a hive. As soon as a good place is found, the old queen flies to it, followed by thousands of workers. This flying mass of bees out to start a new colony is called a *swarm.* Bees usually swarm and build new hives in the spring.

A large swarm of honeybees may contain as many as 10,000 bees!

Queenly Duties

At the old hive, one new queen gets rid of all the others. There is room for only one queen in each hive. Then the new queen flies out, chased by the drones. The drones that catch and mate with her become the fathers of all the eggs that will be laid in the queen's lifetime.

A drone's life is easy, but it is also short. Soon after the queen has mated, the drones are turned away from the hive. Without the workers to feed them, the drones quickly die. The queen, however, is treated royally when she returns to the hive. The workers pamper her and protect her as she begins to lay her eggs.

Amazing as it may seem, a queen can lay up to 1,500 eggs in a single day. Over her lifetime, she may lay more than one million eggs! She lays them, one in each special nursery cell, and then has nothing more to do with them.

The queen bee (center) lays one egg in the bottom of each cell.

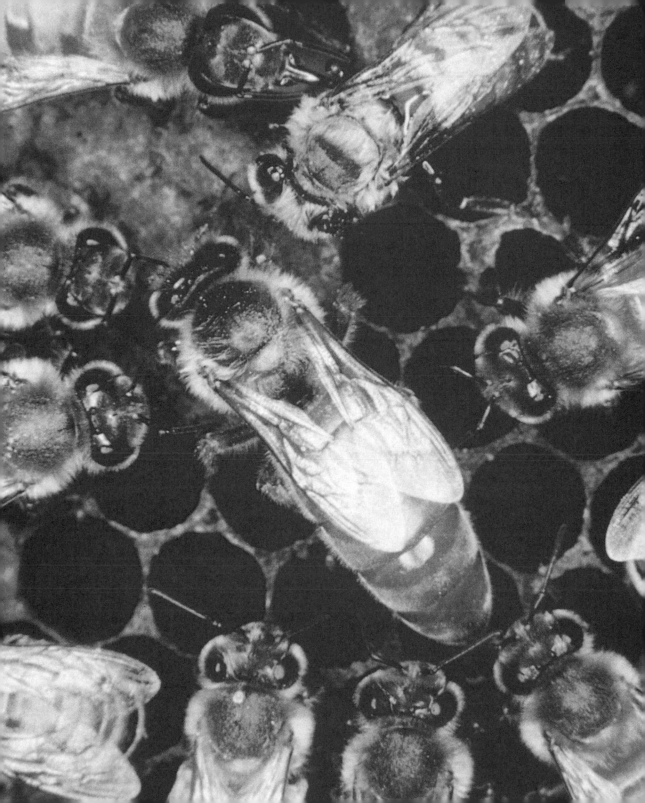

Baby Boomers

Bee eggs are so tiny that one of them could fit on the dot of this "i." After just three days, a little white *grub,* also called a *larva,* hatches out of each egg. These worm-like creatures don't look like adult bees—they don't have wings or legs or even proper heads.

The grubs are fed immediately by worker bees. They eat so much that they grow to adult size in just six days. Royal jelly is the secret to the grubs' amazing growth. Queen grubs eat royal jelly for six days straight. Worker and drone grubs are fed it for only three days. For the next three days, they eat a watery mixture of honey and pollen.

Looking after grubs is no easy task for the worker bees. Each grub has to be fed 1,300 times a day!

A Rest Before Hatching

After their six-day feast, the grubs are sealed into their nursery cells by worker bees. Inside these cozy rooms, the grubs spin themselves *cocoons,* or coverings, and begin to change into adult bees.

The workers make sure the temperature of the hive is just right for the grubs. If the hive cools down, thousands of workers huddle together to warm it up. If it gets too warm, the workers sprinkle water on the cells and fan them with their wings.

In less than two weeks, the grubs become adult bees. They tear open their nursery cells and pop out, fully grown.

These bee grubs are about to emerge as young adults.

Bee of all Trades

Opposite page:
In its short life, a honeybee collects enough nectar to make about six tea-spoons of honey.

Most of the hatching honeybees are females. They will become the worker bees of the hive and have many jobs—construction worker, janitor, nurse, security guard, and food finder.

For the first three weeks, the new worker bees help out inside the hive. They clean cells, feed grubs, make wax for building and repairing the honeycombs, or become guards at the hive entrances.

After about three weeks the young bees may leave the hive and search for food. They start by making short flights close to the hive until they learn how to find their way back home from faraway locations.

Being a worker bee is such hard work that most of them look scruffy by the time they are only four weeks old. Although the workers that are born in the fall usually live through the winter, workers born in spring and summer rarely live more than six weeks.

Good to the Last Drop

How often have you poked your nose into a flower only to find yourself face to face with a bee? You stopped only for a sniff, but the bee was there for a tasty meal! Everything a bee needs to eat can be found inside a flower.

Try plucking a clover blossom and nibbling the base of its petals. What do you taste? Something very sweet? This sugary juice is called *nectar*. In some flowers the nectar is hard to reach. But the bee is well prepared for this. It has a built-in, straw-like drinking tube called a *proboscis*. Just as you use a straw to slurp up those last delicious drops of a soda, a bee uses its proboscis to suck up the tiny nectar droplets.

A honeybee worker carries most of the nectar back to the hive in its stomach. Instead of having just one stomach as we do, a bee has two. It uses one stomach to digest some of the nectar for food for itself. The rest goes back to the hive in a special *honey stomach,* the other of a bee's two stomachs, used only for carrying nectar.

Opposite page: In winter, when there are no flowers to provide nectar, honeybees live on the honey they stored up during the warm months.

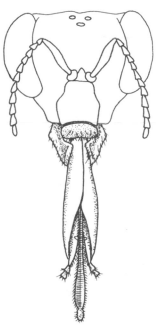

Honeybee proboscis

Honey Factory

As the worker bees fly through fields and gardens, they begin to turn the nectar they have gathered into honey. The nectar is pumped in and out of their honey stomachs where some of the water is removed from the nectar. When the field bees reach the hive, they squirt this sweet liquid into a cell. Other bees then work on the nectar, removing even more water and adding *enzymes,* chemicals produced in their bodies. Finally, when the honey is ready, it is sealed in one of the hive's wax storage cells.

Making honey is no easy task. A bee's honey stomach is little bigger than a grain of rice, and it may take as many as 1,000 flower visits to fill it. To make just one thimbleful of honey, a single bee probably works ten hours a day for six days straight. That's hard work!

The worker bee at the top deposits nectar after returning to the hive. Then other worker bees take over the next step in making honey.

Pollen Baskets

The honeybee is one of nature's most valuable gardeners. To make seeds, many flowers can't use their own *pollen*. Pollen is a sticky powder that flowers produce. The flowers must get the pollen from other flowers—but how, since flowers can't move around?

Each time a bee visits a flower, some of the flower's powdery pollen gets caught in the hair on the bee's body and legs. The bee then spreads this pollen from flower to flower. Bees' work of spreading pollen is so important that some farmers put hives in orchards, fields, and gardens so that the bees and flowers are close together.

Pollen is also part of the bees' baby food. Using a built-in comb and brush on its legs, the bee collects the pollen from her hair and mouth parts. She then carries the pollen back to the hive in pollen baskets located on her hind legs.

With pollen baskets full, this honeybee will soon head for home.

Dance Directions

When you make an exciting discovery, you use words to tell your friends about it. When a bee finds a new patch of sweet flowers, it *dances* to pass on its message to other bees in the hive. A honeybee dance has two features: a round dance and a waggle. The bee does a round dance in the shape of a circle or a figure 8 to show the direction of the flowers in relation to the sun. The bee indicates the distance by waggling its body.

As the bee begins to dance, the other bees study her movements, smell the hairs on her body, and taste the nectar she has collected. From these clues they'll know what kind of flowers to look for and where.

First, those closest to the dancer join in the frenzied dance. Soon a long train of bees dances behind the leader to pass the message on. But the bees don't need to follow the dancer to the new flower patch. After they've been given the dance directions, they can make a beeline for the flowers all by themselves.

Opposite page: *The dancing honeybee shown here with fluttering wings is giving directions to the other bees.*

Silent Scent Signals

Bees have another way of communicating besides dancing. They send scent messages for other bees to smell. They use special scents to mark their hives and warn trespassers to stay out. The queen produces another scent to tell the drones when she is ready to mate. And if you have ever been stung by a bee, you were probably marked by a bee's scent message, too. It warned other bees to be careful—YOU were dangerous!

Anytime you see a bee on a flower, you can be sure it's a female. Only female bees work.

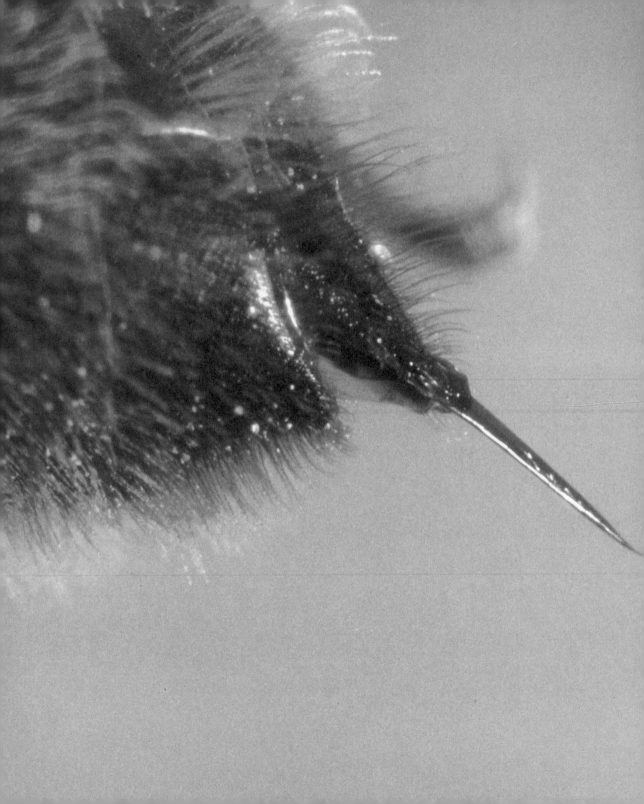

Ouch!

Being stung by a bee will hurt you—and it'll probably kill the bee. The bee's tiny stinger gets hooked so firmly in your skin that the bee tears its body when it tries to fly away. The bee dies after losing its stinger.

When it stings, the bee leaves a tiny drop of *venom*, or poison, under your skin. It's the venom that causes the puffy, itchy, red spot on your skin.

Some people think that bees sting because they're naturally bad tempered, but this is not true. A bee will sting only if it's caught or hurt or if it feels that the hive is in danger. The main danger comes from other animals that want to get at the sweet treat inside the hive.

Bears, skunks, and even "robber" bees from other colonies will brave a stinging for a tasty honey lunch. To warn of an attack, the hive has guard bees. They stand at the hive entrances, and use their antennae to pick up any strange vibrations or odors. If the guards sense danger, they quickly pass the message through the hive and a counterattack begins.

Opposite page: A honeybee uses its stinger as a weapon to defend its colony. Only females have stingers.

Worker bee's stinger

Venom duct

Barbs

Honeybees Forever!

Honeybees will fight to protect their queen and their hive. They'll even die to make sure their hive is safe. These little creatures are among the most determined and organized of the whole animal kingdom.

As we've seen, every honeybee in the hive has its own job to do. The queen lays eggs so that there will always be bees to take care of the hive. In another part of the hive, the drones wait for food and the next queen's mating flight. And the tireless little worker bees buzz endlessly in and out and around the hive. Out to the flowers they fly and back again to store the thick sweet food that has made them famous—honey. Mmm, mmm— long live the honeybee colonies of the world!

Words To Know

Abdomen   The egg-shaped section at the end of a bee's body.

Antennae   A pair of sensitive feelers on the top of a bee's head.

Cocoon   The silky covering that a bee grub spins around itself.

Cells   Six-sided wax "rooms" to raise young bees and hold honey.

Colony   A group of bees that live together in a hive.

Drone   A male bee.

Enzyme   A chemical produced by a living body.

Exoskeleton   The hard outer covering that forms a bee's body.

Gland   A part of the body that makes and gives out a substance.

Grub   A baby bee, also called a larva.

Hive   A bee's home.

Honeycomb   Rows of wax cells in a bee hive.

Honey stomach   A bee's special stomach, for carrying nectar.

Mate   To come together to produce young.

Nectar   A sweet juice that is produced by flowers.

Pollen   A sticky powder on flowers, used to produce seeds.

Proboscis   Hollow tube on a bee's mouth, for sucking up nectar.

Queen   The leader of a bee colony and the one who lays the eggs.

Royal jelly   A special baby food fed to bee grubs.

Swarm   A large group of bees starting a new colony.

Venom   A poison that a bee leaves when stinging.

Workers   Female bees who care for the hive and gather food.

Index

abdomen, 6, 18
antennae, 9, 10, 45

body temperature, 14

cells, 18, 26, 30, 36
clustering, 14, 30, 41
cocoon, 30
cold weather, 13, 14
communication, 41, 42, 45
construction work, 22, 32

dancing, 41
defense, 6, 42, 45
diet, 35
    of grubs, 29, 39
drone, 5, 18, 22, 26, 42, 46

eggs, 22, 25, 26, 29, 46
enemies, 6, 45
exoskeleton, 6
eyes, 9, 22

feeding, 26, 29. 32
feet, 18
flying, 13, 17, 22
food storage cells, 18, 36

gathering food, 5, 22, 32
grub, 29, 30
guards, 32, 45

hairs, 9, 10, 39, 41
head, 6, 22
hive, 5, 18, 22, 25, 36
honey production, 35, 36, 46
housecleaning, 22, 32

larva: *see* grub
legs, 6, 29, 39
life span, 26, 32

mating, 22, 26, 42, 46
mouth, 18, 39

nectar, 35, 41
nursery cells, 26, 30

pollen, 29, 39
proboscis, 35

queen, 5, 18, 22, 25, 26, 42, 46

royal jelly, 25, 29

scent messages, 42
scouts, 25
senses, 9, 10, 13, 45
shape, 6, 22
size, 22
smelling, 41, 42, 45
spring, 25
stinging, 6, 42, 45
stomach, 35
stripes, 6
swarm, 25

thorax, 6,

venom, 45

wax, 18, 32
wings, 17, 29, 30
worker, 5, 18, 22, 25, 29, 30, 32,
    35, 46

PHOTO CREDITS
Cover: Robert C. Simpson, *Valan Photos.* **Interiors:** *Tom Stack & Associates:* D. Wilder, 4, 31;
Gary Milburn, 11; Jeff Foott, 19. /V.Claerhout, 7. /Bill Ivy, 8, 15, 16, 23, 28, 33, 34, 38, 43, 44.
/Maslowski Photo, 12. /*Visuals Unlimited:* J. Alcock, 24; C. Johansen, 27; R. Williamson, 37.
/*Ivy Images:* Norman R. Lightfoot, 40.